Advanced Fine-Tuning Techniques for AI Models: The Most Up To Date Fine Tuning Methods Currently Published

Written By Richard Aragon

Introduction to Advanced Fine-Tuning Techniques for AI Models

In the rapidly evolving landscape of artificial intelligence, the ability to adapt and refine pre-trained models for specific tasks and domains has become a cornerstone of AI research and application. This book delves into the cutting-edge of fine-tuning techniques, offering a comprehensive guide to harnessing the full potential of AI models across a wide array of disciplines.

As the complexity and capabilities of AI models, particularly in natural language processing and computer vision, have grown, so too have the strategies for their optimization. Traditional approaches to training AI models from scratch are increasingly supplanted by more sophisticated fine-tuning methods. These methods not only enhance model performance on specialized tasks but also significantly reduce the time and resources required for training.

This book is designed to serve both as an introduction to newcomers in the field and as a detailed guide for experienced practitioners. It encompasses a broad spectrum of fine-tuning techniques, from the foundational principles of transfer learning to the latest innovations in model adaptation and optimization.

Structure of the Book

The book is structured to provide a logical progression through the various aspects of fine-tuning, starting with basic concepts and moving towards more advanced and specialized techniques. Each chapter is dedicated to a specific method or aspect of fine-tuning, including detailed explanations of the underlying theory, practical applications, and case studies highlighting real-world implementations.

1. Foundational Concepts: We begin with an overview of machine learning fundamentals, focusing on the principles of transfer learning and the rationale behind fine-tuning pre-trained models.
2. Technique-Specific Chapters: The core of the book is a series of chapters each dedicated to a different fine-tuning technique. These chapters delve into the mechanics, advantages, and challenges of each method, supported by examples and comparative analyses.
3. Cross-Disciplinary Applications: The book explores the application of fine-tuning techniques across various domains, including natural language processing, computer vision, and beyond, showcasing the versatility and impact of these methods.
4. Practical Considerations: Beyond theoretical insights, the book addresses practical aspects of fine-tuning, such as computational requirements, data preparation, and toolkits, equipping readers with the knowledge to implement these techniques effectively.
5. Future Directions: We conclude with a forward-looking perspective on the evolution of fine-tuning techniques, discussing emerging trends, potential research directions, and the broader implications for the field of artificial intelligence.

Audience

This book is intended for a broad audience, including students, researchers, and professionals in the field of artificial intelligence. Whether you are seeking to deepen your understanding of advanced fine-tuning techniques or looking for practical advice on applying these methods to your projects, this book offers valuable insights and guidance.

Objective

Our aim is to demystify the process of fine-tuning AI models, providing readers with the tools and knowledge to push the boundaries of what is possible with artificial intelligence. By exploring the depth and breadth of fine-tuning techniques, we hope to inspire innovation and advance the state of the art in AI research and application.

Welcome to the journey through the fascinating world of fine-tuning AI models. Let this book be your guide to mastering the art and science of optimizing artificial intelligence to meet the challenges of tomorrow.

Chapter 1: Introduction to Fine-Tuning in Machine Learning

1.1 Overview of Machine Learning Models

Machine learning models are computational algorithms that learn patterns from data. These models can be broadly categorized into three types: supervised learning, where models predict an output based on input data; unsupervised learning, where models identify patterns or structures in data without any labels; and reinforcement learning, where models learn to make decisions by receiving feedback from their environment. At the heart of these models are neural networks, especially deep learning models, which have layers of interconnected nodes that mimic the neural connections in the human brain. These networks can learn complex representations of data, making them incredibly powerful tools for a wide range of applications, from image and speech recognition to natural language processing and beyond.

1.2 The Evolution of Fine-Tuning

The concept of fine-tuning in machine learning has evolved significantly over the past decade. Initially, models were trained from scratch for each new task, requiring substantial amounts of data and computational resources. The introduction of transfer learning marked a pivotal change, where a model pretrained on a large dataset could be adapted or "fine-tuned" for a specific task with comparatively less data. This approach leveraged the knowledge the model had already acquired, significantly reducing the need for extensive computational resources and large labeled datasets for every new task.

As machine learning models, particularly deep learning networks, have grown in complexity and capacity, fine-tuning has become an essential technique for customizing models to specific domains or tasks. This has led to the development of sophisticated fine-tuning methodologies, including few-shot learning, zero-shot learning, and domain-specific tuning, that further refine the model's ability to adapt to new data with minimal supervision.

1.3 Importance of Fine-Tuning in Modern AI

Fine-tuning has become a cornerstone of modern AI, enabling the rapid deployment of highly specialized models across a variety of domains. It allows for the customization of general-purpose models to specific tasks, improving their performance, efficiency, and applicability. In the era of big data, where data availability can vary widely across tasks, fine-tuning offers a practical solution to leverage existing knowledge and reduce the resources required for model training.

Moreover, fine-tuning plays a critical role in the democratization of AI, making state-of-the-art models accessible to a broader range of users and organizations. By allowing for the efficient adaptation of pretrained models, fine-tuning lowers the barrier to entry for developing sophisticated AI applications, fostering innovation and expanding the potential uses of AI technology.

Furthermore, as AI systems are increasingly deployed in dynamic and evolving environments, fine-tuning offers a mechanism for models to be updated and improved over time. This adaptability is crucial for maintaining the relevance and effectiveness of AI systems in the face of changing data landscapes, emerging trends, and new challenges.

In summary, fine-tuning not only enhances the performance and efficiency of machine learning models but also plays a pivotal role in expanding the scope and accessibility of AI technologies. Its continued development and application promise to drive further advancements and innovations in the field of AI.

Chapter 2: Fundamental Concepts of Fine-Tuning

2.1 Transfer Learning

Transfer learning is a machine learning method where a model developed for one task is reused as the starting point for a model on a second task. It is a popular approach in deep learning where pretrained models are leveraged to solve similar but distinct problems. This technique is particularly useful because it allows for the utilization of knowledge gained while solving one problem and applying it to different but related problems. Transfer learning has two main benefits: it can significantly reduce the time and computational resources required to develop machine learning models, and it can improve model performance when the amount of data available for the new task is limited.

2.2 Few-Shot Learning

Few-shot learning refers to the ability of a model to learn and generalize from a very small dataset. In the context of fine-tuning, few-shot learning techniques are applied to adapt a model to new tasks with minimal examples. This is especially important in scenarios where collecting large amounts of labeled data is impractical or expensive. Few-shot learning relies heavily on the quality of the pretrained model and the effectiveness of the fine-tuning process, utilizing advanced strategies like meta-learning, where the model is trained on a variety of tasks to improve its ability to adapt quickly to new tasks with few examples.

2.3 Zero-Shot Learning

Zero-shot learning takes the concept of few-shot learning further by enabling models to perform tasks without having seen any examples of that specific task during training. This is achieved by transferring knowledge from related tasks and leveraging rich semantic representations. Zero-shot learning is particularly relevant for tasks where it is impossible to obtain labeled data for every potential class or scenario. In practice, this involves training models on a diverse set of tasks or using embeddings that capture a wide range of concepts, allowing the model to make inferences about unseen classes based on learned relationships and similarities.

2.4 The Role of Pretrained Models

Pretrained models are the backbone of fine-tuning in modern machine learning. These models, which are often trained on vast datasets, capture a wide range of features and patterns that can be leveraged for a variety of tasks. The role of pretrained models in fine-tuning is multifaceted: they provide a rich feature extraction mechanism, reduce the need for large domain-specific datasets, and serve as a universal starting point for customizing models to specific tasks.

Pretraining followed by fine-tuning has become a standard approach in many AI applications, including natural language processing, computer vision, and speech recognition. The effectiveness of this approach is evident in the widespread use of models like BERT for text,

ResNet for images, and Wav2Vec for audio. These models, once fine-tuned, can achieve state-of-the-art performance on specific tasks with only a fraction of the training data and time that would be required to train a model from scratch.

In summary, the fundamental concepts of fine-tuning, including transfer learning, few-shot learning, zero-shot learning, and the utilization of pretrained models, form the foundation of modern machine learning practices. By leveraging these techniques, researchers and practitioners can develop highly specialized and efficient models, pushing the boundaries of what's possible with AI.

Chapter 3: QLORA - Quantum Logic Reinforced Attention

3.1 Introduction to Quantum Computing in AI

Quantum computing represents a paradigm shift in computation, utilizing the principles of quantum mechanics to process information in ways that are fundamentally different from classical computing. In the realm of artificial intelligence (AI), quantum computing offers the potential to solve complex problems more efficiently than traditional computers, particularly in areas such as optimization, simulation, and machine learning. Quantum algorithms can process vast amounts of data simultaneously through quantum parallelism, potentially enabling AI systems to achieve new levels of performance and capability.

3.2 The Concept and Mechanism of QLORA

QLORA, or Quantum Logic Reinforced Attention, is an innovative approach that combines quantum computing principles with deep learning techniques, specifically in the context of attention mechanisms in neural networks. Attention mechanisms have revolutionized fields like natural language processing and computer vision by allowing models to focus on the most relevant parts of the input data. QLORA enhances this by incorporating quantum logic, which can represent and process complex patterns and relationships in data at a quantum level.

The mechanism of QLORA involves using quantum circuits to perform attention calculations, exploiting the superposition and entanglement properties of quantum bits (qubits) to analyze and weigh the importance of different parts of the input data more efficiently than classical attention mechanisms. This can lead to significant improvements in both the speed and accuracy of AI models, as QLORA can theoretically evaluate all possible combinations of data points simultaneously.

3.3 Applications and Case Studies

QLORA's potential applications span across various domains where attention mechanisms are critical. In natural language processing, QLORA can enhance language models, enabling more nuanced understanding and generation of text by efficiently processing and prioritizing information in large datasets. In computer vision, QLORA could improve object detection and image classification by more effectively focusing on relevant features within images.

Case studies demonstrating QLORA's effectiveness include its application in drug discovery, where it has been used to analyze molecular structures and interactions at a quantum level, significantly speeding up the identification of potential drug candidates. Another case study involves the use of QLORA in financial modeling, where it has helped to more accurately predict market trends by analyzing vast amounts of financial data with quantum-enhanced attention to detail.

3.4 Future Directions of QLORA

The future of QLORA is closely tied to advancements in both quantum computing and AI. As quantum hardware continues to evolve and become more accessible, the implementation of QLORA and similar quantum-enhanced AI techniques will likely become more widespread, unlocking new possibilities across various fields.

Research is ongoing into how QLORA can be further optimized and integrated with other quantum computing and AI advancements, such as quantum machine learning algorithms and hybrid quantum-classical systems. Additionally, exploring the ethical and societal implications of quantum-enhanced AI, including issues of data privacy, security, and the potential impact on employment and society, will be crucial as these technologies develop.

In conclusion, QLORA stands at the intersection of quantum computing and AI, offering a glimpse into the future of how these technologies can converge to solve complex problems more efficiently. Its development and application will not only advance the field of AI but also highlight the transformative potential of quantum computing in enhancing and revolutionizing various domains.

Chapter 4: LASER - Language-Agnostic SEntence Representations

4.1 Background and Development

The development of LASER (Language-Agnostic SEntence Representations) marks a significant advancement in the field of natural language processing (NLP). Traditional NLP models often struggled with cross-lingual tasks due to the need for separate models for each language, leading to increased complexity and resource requirements. LASER was introduced as a solution to this problem, offering a single model capable of understanding and processing multiple languages with high efficiency.

The background of LASER lies in the recognition of the importance of creating scalable, efficient models that can handle the diversity of global languages without compromising on performance. Developed by researchers aiming to break the language barriers in NLP, LASER focuses on creating a universal representation of sentences across languages, enabling seamless translation, sentiment analysis, and other language tasks without the need for language-specific models.

4.2 How LASER Works

LASER works by encoding sentences into high-dimensional vectors, regardless of the original language. This is achieved through a deep learning architecture that combines several key components: a Byte Pair Encoding (BPE) for handling subword units across languages, a bidirectional Long Short-Term Memory (BiLSTM) network for encoding the sequences, and a self-attention mechanism to capture the context within sentences.

The process begins with the tokenization of sentences into subword units, allowing the model to efficiently process linguistic similarities across languages. The BiLSTM network then processes these tokens, capturing both the forward and backward context of each subword in a sentence. Finally, the self-attention mechanism aggregates this information, producing a single vector representation for each sentence. These vectors are language-agnostic, meaning they capture the semantic essence of the sentence regardless of the input language.

4.3 Advantages Over Traditional Models

The primary advantage of LASER over traditional models is its language-agnostic capability, which enables it to perform NLP tasks across languages without the need for individual language-specific models. This not only simplifies the model architecture but also significantly reduces the resources required for training and deploying NLP systems across different linguistic contexts.

Furthermore, LASER's ability to encode sentences into dense vectors that capture deep semantic meanings allows for more nuanced understanding and processing of language. This results in improved performance on a range of tasks, including text classification, translation, and information extraction, especially in scenarios involving multiple languages.

4.4 Use Cases and Applications

LASER has a wide array of applications across various domains. In translation services, LASER can be used to develop efficient, high-quality translation systems that support multiple languages with a single model, greatly enhancing accessibility and user experience. In content moderation, LASER's ability to understand the semantic content of sentences enables more effective filtering and moderation of multilingual content.

Another significant application is in cross-lingual sentiment analysis, where businesses and researchers can gain insights into the sentiments of users across different languages without the need for separate models. This has profound implications for global market research, social media analysis, and customer feedback systems.

In conclusion, LASER represents a major leap forward in the quest for truly global NLP systems. By providing a universal, language-agnostic method for sentence representation, LASER not only simplifies the process of developing multilingual NLP applications but also opens up new possibilities for understanding and interacting with language on a global scale.

Chapter 5: ITL - Interactive Transfer Learning

5.1 Understanding Interactive Learning

Interactive Learning is a paradigm within machine learning where models learn and adapt through interaction with their environment or feedback from humans. Unlike traditional learning approaches that rely on static datasets, interactive learning enables models to dynamically improve by incorporating new data or corrections in real-time. This approach is particularly effective for tasks where automated systems must adapt to changing conditions or where human expertise can significantly enhance model performance.

5.2 Integrating Transfer Learning with Interactive Techniques

Interactive Transfer Learning (ITL) merges the concept of transfer learning with interactive learning to create a powerful framework for building adaptable AI systems. Transfer learning, the process of applying knowledge gained from one task to solve related tasks, provides a strong foundation by leveraging pre-existing models and data. When combined with interactive learning, it allows these systems to not only start with a high level of understanding but also continuously evolve through interactions.

ITL involves fine-tuning pretrained models on a specific task with the added dimension of human-in-the-loop feedback mechanisms. This integration enables models to quickly adapt to new domains or tasks with minimal data, while also refining their understanding based on real-world usage and feedback. It represents a significant step towards creating more flexible, efficient, and user-centered AI systems.

5.3 Practical Applications and Success Stories

One of the key applications of ITL has been in natural language processing (NLP), where models like chatbots or language translators continuously improve their understanding and responses based on user interactions. For example, a chatbot trained on general conversation can be quickly adapted to provide technical support through ITL, learning from each interaction to better respond to user inquiries over time.

In the medical field, ITL has been used to enhance diagnostic models. By integrating expert feedback into the learning process, these models can improve their diagnostic accuracy, adapting to new findings or variations in medical data that were not part of their initial training set.

Another success story comes from robotics, where ITL has enabled robots to learn and adapt to new tasks through interaction with their environment or guidance from human operators. This approach has significantly accelerated the pace at which robots can be repurposed for new tasks, enhancing their usefulness in dynamic environments.

5.4 Challenges and Opportunities

While ITL offers significant advantages, it also presents challenges. The quality of the interactive feedback is crucial; inaccurate or biased feedback can lead models astray. Additionally, designing systems that can effectively incorporate real-time feedback without compromising performance or privacy is a technical challenge.

Despite these challenges, the opportunities presented by ITL are vast. As AI systems become more integrated into daily life, the ability to adapt and learn from human feedback will be critical. ITL offers a pathway to creating AI systems that are not only more responsive to human needs but also capable of growing in intelligence and utility over time.

In conclusion, ITL represents a significant advancement in the development of adaptable, efficient, and user-friendly AI systems. By combining the strengths of transfer learning with interactive learning, ITL paves the way for a new generation of AI applications that can learn and evolve in concert with their human users, opening up endless possibilities for innovation and improvement across various domains.

Chapter 6: Prompt-based Learning and Tuning

6.1 Understanding Prompt-based Learning

Prompt-based learning represents a paradigm shift in how we interact with and guide machine learning models, particularly large language models (LLMs) like GPT-3 and its successors. This approach leverages natural language prompts to direct the model's attention and response generation, making it possible to achieve specific outcomes without extensive retraining or fine-tuning. Prompt-based learning essentially turns the model into a more versatile tool, capable of handling a wide range of tasks with the right prompts.

6.2 The Mechanics of Prompt-based Tuning

At the heart of prompt-based tuning is the strategic use of prompts that are designed to elicit specific types of responses from a model. These prompts can range from simple instructions ("Translate the following text into French:") to more complex, context-rich scenarios that guide the model towards generating outputs in a certain style or tone. The effectiveness of this approach lies in its simplicity and the ability to leverage the vast knowledge encoded within LLMs, making it possible to tailor model outputs to a wide array of tasks without modifying the underlying model architecture or training data.

6.3 Practical Applications and Success Stories

The applications of prompt-based learning are as diverse as the capabilities of the LLMs themselves. In creative writing, prompts are used to generate story ideas, dialogue, or entire narratives in specific genres. In the field of education, teachers use prompts to create customized tutoring sessions that help students explore complex topics. For businesses, prompt-based learning has been instrumental in generating marketing content, summarizing reports, and even drafting emails or communications in a specific corporate voice.

One notable success story involves using GPT-3 for legal document analysis, where prompts guide the model to extract relevant details and summarize complex legal language, making it accessible to non-experts. Another example is in programming, where developers use prompts to generate code snippets or debug existing code, significantly speeding up the development process.

6.4 Challenges and Opportunities

Despite its flexibility and power, prompt-based learning is not without challenges. Crafting effective prompts is an art that requires a deep understanding of the model's capabilities and limitations. There is also the issue of prompt engineering, where finding the right prompt can become a time-consuming process, especially for complex tasks. Moreover, the reliability of the generated content can vary, necessitating careful review and, at times, manual correction.

However, the opportunities presented by prompt-based learning and tuning are immense. As models continue to evolve, becoming more sophisticated and capable, the range of tasks they can perform with simple guidance expands. This opens up new avenues for personalized AI assistance, creative content generation, and even complex problem-solving in domains previously thought to be exclusive to human expertise.

In conclusion, prompt-based learning and tuning stand out as a highly adaptable and user-friendly approach to leveraging the power of large language models. By understanding and mastering the art of prompt engineering, users can unlock the full potential of these models, pushing the boundaries of what's possible with AI and opening up a world of creative and practical applications.

Chapter 7: Diffusion Models for Fine-Tuning

7.1 Introduction to Diffusion Models

Diffusion models have emerged as a powerful class of generative models that produce high-quality data samples, such as images or audio, by gradually denoising a random noise signal over a series of steps. This process is inspired by the physical process of diffusion, which is essentially reversed to generate data from noise. Unlike traditional generative models that directly output data samples, diffusion models iteratively refine their outputs, leading to high-fidelity and diverse creations.

7.2 The Role of Diffusion Models in Fine-Tuning

In the context of fine-tuning, diffusion models offer a novel approach to improving and customizing pre-trained models for specific tasks. By integrating diffusion processes, researchers can fine-tune models on a target dataset to generate outputs that closely match the desired characteristics and quality. This approach is particularly beneficial for applications requiring high levels of detail and realism, such as image synthesis, speech generation, and even music production.

7.3 Applications and Case Studies

The application of diffusion models for fine-tuning has shown promising results across various domains:

- Image Synthesis: Fine-tuning diffusion models on specific image datasets allows for the creation of highly detailed and realistic images, from portraits to landscapes. This approach has been used to generate artwork and design elements that are indistinguishable from those created by humans.

- Speech Synthesis: In speech synthesis, diffusion models fine-tuned on specific voices or accents can generate natural-sounding speech that captures the nuances of the target audio. This technology has applications in virtual assistants, audiobooks, and language learning tools, where personalized or highly realistic speech is crucial.

- Music Production: Diffusion models have also been applied to generate music, where they can be fine-tuned on specific genres or artists' styles to create new compositions. This opens up new possibilities for personalized music creation and exploration of novel musical landscapes.

7.4 Challenges and Opportunities

While diffusion models for fine-tuning hold immense potential, they also present unique challenges. The computational complexity of running multiple denoising steps makes the fine-tuning and generation processes resource-intensive, requiring significant computational power. Additionally, controlling the output to ensure that it aligns with specific requirements or constraints remains a complex task that often requires careful tuning of the model and the generation process.

Despite these challenges, the opportunities presented by diffusion models for fine-tuning are vast. As computational resources become more accessible and techniques for controlling and guiding the generation process improve, diffusion models could revolutionize the way we create and interact with digital content. From creating personalized content on demand to advancing the realism of synthetic media, diffusion models stand at the forefront of the next wave of innovations in generative AI.

In conclusion, diffusion models for fine-tuning represent a cutting-edge approach to generating high-fidelity and highly customized digital content. By leveraging the unique capabilities of these models, researchers and practitioners can push the boundaries of creativity and realism in digital media, opening up new frontiers in image and speech synthesis, music production, and beyond.

Chapter 8: Meta-Learning for Fine-Tuning

8.1 The Concept of Meta-Learning

Meta-learning, often described as "learning to learn," is a paradigm in machine learning that focuses on designing models and algorithms capable of quickly adapting to new tasks with minimal data. Unlike traditional learning approaches that aim to optimize performance on a specific task, meta-learning aims to optimize the learning process itself, enabling a model to learn new tasks more efficiently. This approach is particularly valuable in scenarios where data is scarce or where models need to be rapidly adapted across diverse domains.

8.2 Meta-Learning in the Context of Fine-Tuning

In the fine-tuning process, meta-learning offers a transformative approach by allowing pre-trained models to leverage their existing knowledge and quickly adapt to new tasks or datasets. This is achieved through techniques that adjust the model's learning algorithm, enabling it to learn from a few examples or even a single example (few-shot learning). Meta-learning techniques, such as Model-Agnostic Meta-Learning (MAML) or Reptile, are designed to find optimal initialization parameters for a model so that it can effectively adapt to a new task with just a few gradient updates.

8.3 Applications and Success Stories

Meta-learning has found applications across a wide range of fields, demonstrating its versatility and effectiveness in enhancing fine-tuning processes:

- Few-Shot Learning: In scenarios where labeled data is limited, meta-learning enables models to achieve high accuracy with minimal examples. This is particularly useful in specialized domains like medical image diagnosis, where acquiring large annotated datasets can be challenging.

- Natural Language Processing (NLP): Meta-learning has been applied to adapt NLP models to new languages or dialects quickly, improving the model's performance on translation, sentiment analysis, and other language tasks with limited training data.

- Reinforcement Learning: Meta-learning has enhanced the ability of reinforcement learning models to adapt to new environments or rules more efficiently, accelerating the learning process in complex simulation environments and real-world applications like robotics.

8.4 Challenges and Opportunities

While meta-learning offers significant advantages for fine-tuning and rapid adaptation to new tasks, it also presents challenges. Designing meta-learning algorithms that are both efficient and effective requires careful consideration of the balance between adaptability and overfitting.

Additionally, the computational complexity of some meta-learning approaches can be high, necessitating efficient implementation and optimization techniques.

However, the opportunities presented by meta-learning for fine-tuning are vast. As research in this area continues to evolve, we can expect to see more sophisticated meta-learning algorithms that can further reduce the data requirements for training models and enhance their adaptability. This could lead to breakthroughs in personalized AI services, where models can quickly adjust to individual user preferences or needs, and in developing AI systems capable of tackling a broader range of tasks with minimal human intervention.

In conclusion, meta-learning represents a frontier in the development of more flexible and efficient AI systems. By enabling models to learn how to learn, meta-learning for fine-tuning opens up new possibilities for creating AI that can quickly adapt across a myriad of tasks and domains, paving the way for more personalized, adaptable, and efficient AI solutions.

Chapter 9: Adversarial Fine-Tuning

9.1 Introduction to Adversarial Training

Adversarial training is a technique in machine learning designed to improve the robustness of models by exposing them to adversarial examples during the training phase. These adversarial examples are inputs that have been slightly modified in a way that is intended to deceive the model into making incorrect predictions or classifications. The goal of adversarial training is to make models more resilient against such deceptive inputs, enhancing their security and reliability, especially in applications where AI systems can be subject to malicious attacks.

9.2 Incorporating Adversarial Concepts in Fine-Tuning

Adversarial fine-tuning integrates the principles of adversarial training into the fine-tuning process of pre-trained models. By doing so, it aims to achieve two primary objectives: improving the model's generalization capabilities and enhancing its robustness against adversarial attacks. This is accomplished by introducing adversarial examples as part of the fine-tuning dataset, forcing the model to learn to correctly classify not only benign inputs but also those that have been intentionally perturbed. This method not only hardens the model against potential attacks but also often leads to improved performance on standard inputs by encouraging the model to learn more generalizable features.

9.3 Applications and Case Studies

The application of adversarial fine-tuning spans various domains, highlighting its effectiveness in enhancing model security and reliability:

- Computer Vision: In image recognition and object detection, adversarial fine-tuning helps models resist attacks designed to manipulate their predictions by subtly altering input images. This is critical for applications like autonomous driving and surveillance, where reliability is paramount.

- Natural Language Processing (NLP): For NLP tasks such as sentiment analysis and text classification, adversarial fine-tuning improves the model's ability to handle deceptive or manipulated text, ensuring more reliable analysis and decision-making.

- Cybersecurity: In detecting malicious software or phishing attempts, models fine-tuned with adversarial examples can better identify subtle, malicious alterations designed to bypass traditional detection methods.

9.4 Challenges and Opportunities

While adversarial fine-tuning significantly enhances model robustness, it also presents challenges. Generating effective adversarial examples that lead to meaningful learning without causing excessive computational overhead is a complex task. Additionally, there is always a risk of overfitting to the adversarial examples used during training, potentially reducing the model's performance on genuine inputs.

However, the opportunities for advancing AI security and reliability through adversarial fine-tuning are substantial. Continued research and development in this area could lead to the creation of AI systems that are not only more resistant to attacks but also exhibit improved generalization across tasks. This is particularly relevant in sectors where AI decision-making is critical, such as healthcare, finance, and national security.

In conclusion, adversarial fine-tuning represents a vital step forward in the quest to develop AI systems that are both robust and reliable. By incorporating adversarial examples into the fine-tuning process, models can be better prepared to handle the increasingly sophisticated attacks they may face in the real world, ensuring their safe and effective deployment across a wide range of applications.

Chapter 10: Federated Fine-Tuning

10.1 Introduction to Federated Learning

Federated learning is a distributed machine learning approach that allows models to be trained across multiple devices or servers without requiring the data to be centralized. This technique is particularly valuable for scenarios where data privacy, security, and ownership are critical concerns. By keeping the data localized and only sharing model updates (e.g., gradients or parameters) across the network, federated learning offers a privacy-preserving alternative to traditional centralized training methods.

10.2 Federated Fine-Tuning: Principles and Mechanisms

Federated fine-tuning extends the principles of federated learning to the fine-tuning process of pre-trained models. Instead of fine-tuning a model on a centralized dataset, federated fine-tuning involves distributing the task across multiple nodes, each with its own local data. These nodes independently perform fine-tuning tasks on their local data and then share their model updates with a central server or aggregator. The aggregator combines these updates to improve the global model, which is then distributed back to the nodes for further training. This process iterates, with the model gradually improving with each cycle.

10.3 Applications and Impact

Federated fine-tuning has significant implications for a wide range of applications, especially in fields where data privacy is paramount:

- Healthcare: Patient data can be highly sensitive, making federated fine-tuning an attractive option for developing personalized medicine applications or diagnostic tools without compromising patient privacy.

- Finance: Financial institutions can use federated fine-tuning to enhance fraud detection systems by leveraging data across multiple branches or entities without sharing sensitive customer information.

- Smart Devices: From smartphones to IoT devices, federated fine-tuning allows manufacturers to improve device functionality (e.g., voice recognition, predictive text) by learning from user interactions without sending sensitive data to a central server.

10.4 Challenges and Future Directions

Implementing federated fine-tuning comes with its own set of challenges. Communication overhead, data heterogeneity across nodes, and ensuring the security of the model updates are significant concerns. Additionally, maintaining the efficiency and accuracy of the global model when it is being fine-tuned across potentially millions of devices with diverse data distributions requires innovative algorithmic solutions.

Despite these challenges, the opportunities presented by federated fine-tuning for enhancing privacy and security in AI applications are vast. Future research is likely to focus on developing more efficient algorithms for aggregating model updates, techniques for dealing with non-IID (independently and identically distributed) data, and methods for ensuring the robustness and security of the federated learning process.

In conclusion, federated fine-tuning represents a pioneering approach to reconciling the need for personalized, data-driven AI applications with the imperative of data privacy and security. As this field evolves, it promises to enable the development of more secure, private, and personalized AI services across a broad spectrum of industries, from healthcare to consumer electronics, thereby expanding the potential for AI to benefit society.

Chapter 11: Cross-Modal Fine-Tuning

11.1 Introduction to Cross-Modal Learning

Cross-modal learning refers to the process of learning that involves more than one type of data modality, such as text, images, audio, or video. The fundamental challenge and opportunity in cross-modal learning lie in effectively integrating and leveraging the distinct types of information that each modality provides. This approach enables AI systems to understand and interpret the world in a more holistic and human-like manner, drawing on multiple sources of information to make decisions or generate outputs.

11.2 Principles of Cross-Modal Fine-Tuning

Cross-modal fine-tuning involves adapting a pre-trained model, typically trained on a single modality, to work effectively across different modalities. This process requires the model to learn representations that are not only relevant within each modality but also transferable across modalities. Techniques such as shared representation learning, where a common embedding space is learned for different modalities, and modality translation, where information from one modality is used to generate or inform processing in another, are key to successful cross-modal fine-tuning.

11.3 Applications and Impact

The versatility of cross-modal fine-tuning has led to significant advancements in a range of applications:

- Multimedia Search: Enhancing search engines to understand queries and content across text, images, and videos, improving the relevance and richness of search results.
- Accessible Technology: Creating more effective tools for individuals with disabilities, such as generating descriptive text for images for the visually impaired or translating speech into text for the hearing impaired.
- Content Creation and Editing: Facilitating more intuitive interfaces for content creation and editing, where users can seamlessly switch between text, audio, and visual modalities to express their ideas.

11.4 Challenges and Opportunities

Cross-modal fine-tuning presents unique challenges, including the need to handle the vastly different feature spaces and distributions that each modality presents and the difficulty of aligning these features into a coherent representation that can be effectively used by the model. Additionally, data scarcity in one or more modalities can limit the effectiveness of cross-modal learning.

Despite these challenges, the opportunities for innovation and impact in this area are vast. Ongoing research is focusing on developing more sophisticated methods for cross-modal representation learning, including deep learning architectures specifically designed to handle multi-modal data and techniques for efficient modality alignment and translation.

Future directions in cross-modal fine-tuning are likely to explore more advanced integration of modalities, such as interactive systems that can engage in dialogues incorporating text, visual input, and other modalities, or autonomous systems that can navigate and interact with the physical world using a combination of sensory inputs.

In conclusion, cross-modal fine-tuning represents a frontier in AI research and application, promising to unlock new capabilities for AI systems to understand and interact with the world in a more integrated and human-like manner. As techniques in this area continue to evolve, we can expect to see increasingly sophisticated and versatile AI systems capable of leveraging the rich, multi-modal nature of human experience and knowledge.

Chapter 12: Energy-Efficient Fine-Tuning

12.1 The Need for Energy Efficiency in AI

The environmental impact of training large-scale artificial intelligence (AI) models has become a significant concern. The computational resources required for training and fine-tuning these models often involve substantial electricity consumption, leading to a large carbon footprint. As AI models become increasingly complex and widespread, finding ways to reduce their energy consumption during the training phase is crucial for sustainable development in the field.

12.2 Principles of Energy-Efficient Fine-Tuning

Energy-efficient fine-tuning involves optimizing the training process to reduce the amount of computational power needed, thereby lowering energy consumption. Several strategies have been developed to achieve this goal:

- Model Pruning: Simplifying the architecture of neural networks by removing neurons or layers that contribute little to the model's performance can significantly reduce computational requirements.
- Quantization: Reducing the precision of the numbers used in the model's computations can decrease the amount of energy needed for training and inference, with minimal impact on performance.
- Knowledge Distillation: Training a smaller, more efficient model to mimic the behavior of a larger, pre-trained model can achieve similar performance with far less energy consumption.
- Efficient Data Sampling: Selectively training on subsets of data or using techniques to prioritize more informative data points can reduce the number of training iterations needed.

12.3 Applications and Impact

Energy-efficient fine-tuning is particularly important in scenarios where computational resources are limited or where minimizing environmental impact is a priority. This approach enables the deployment of advanced AI models on mobile devices, IoT devices, and in remote areas with limited access to power. Moreover, it contributes to the overall sustainability of AI research and application, aligning with global efforts to reduce energy consumption and mitigate climate change.

12.4 Challenges and Future Directions

One of the main challenges in energy-efficient fine-tuning is balancing the trade-off between model performance and energy consumption. While techniques like pruning and quantization can reduce energy use, they may also lead to a decrease in model accuracy or robustness. Future research is focusing on developing new algorithms and training methods that can minimize this trade-off, making it possible to train highly efficient models without significant losses in performance.

Advancements in hardware specifically designed for energy-efficient computations, such as neuromorphic chips and quantum computing, also hold promise for reducing the energy impact of training AI models. Additionally, novel approaches in algorithmic efficiency, such as adaptive training methods that dynamically adjust the model's complexity based on the task, are being explored to further enhance energy efficiency.

In conclusion, energy-efficient fine-tuning represents a critical area of research in the quest to make AI more sustainable and accessible. As the field continues to evolve, these techniques will play a vital role in enabling the widespread adoption of AI technologies while minimizing their environmental footprint.

Chapter 13: Dynamic Fine-Tuning

13.1 Introduction to Dynamic Fine-Tuning

Dynamic fine-tuning represents an advanced approach in the field of machine learning, where the fine-tuning process is adjusted in real-time based on the model's performance on a specific task. Unlike traditional fine-tuning methods that use static parameters and configurations throughout the training process, dynamic fine-tuning adapts various elements such as learning rates, model architecture, and data sampling strategies as the model learns. This adaptability allows for more efficient and effective model optimization, especially for complex tasks or those with evolving data distributions.

13.2 Key Components of Dynamic Fine-Tuning

- Adaptive Learning Rates: Dynamically adjusting the learning rate based on the model's progress can help avoid local minima and ensure more stable convergence.
- Architecture Adjustment: Modifying the model architecture during fine-tuning, such as adding or removing layers, or adjusting the connectivity between neurons, to better fit the specific characteristics of the task.
- Dynamic Data Sampling: Selectively choosing training samples that are most beneficial at different stages of the learning process, focusing on harder examples as the model improves or adjusting the sampling distribution to better match the target task.

13.3 Applications and Impact

Dynamic fine-tuning can significantly improve the performance of AI models across a wide range of applications:

- Personalized AI Systems: For applications like recommendation systems or personalized content delivery, dynamic fine-tuning can adjust models in real-time to fit individual user preferences or changes in behavior patterns.
- Evolving Tasks: In areas where data distributions change over time, such as fraud detection or social media trend analysis, dynamic fine-tuning helps maintain high model performance by continuously adapting to new patterns.
- Resource-Limited Environments: By optimizing the training process, dynamic fine-tuning can reduce computational requirements, making it possible to deploy advanced models on devices with limited processing power.

13.4 Challenges and Future Directions

Implementing dynamic fine-tuning presents several challenges, including the complexity of designing systems that can effectively monitor and adjust their own training processes. There is also a risk of overfitting if the model becomes too specialized to the nuances of the training data at the expense of generalization to unseen data.

Future research in dynamic fine-tuning is likely to explore more sophisticated methods for real-time model adaptation, such as leveraging reinforcement learning to guide the fine-tuning process or developing more advanced metrics for assessing model performance in the context of specific tasks. Additionally, as dynamic fine-tuning becomes more prevalent, there will be an increased need for tools and frameworks that can support these more complex training processes, making them accessible to a wider range of AI practitioners.

In conclusion, dynamic fine-tuning offers a promising path toward creating more adaptable, efficient, and effective AI systems. By enabling models to evolve in response to their performance and the characteristics of their tasks, this approach holds the potential to unlock new levels of AI capabilities, particularly in rapidly changing or highly personalized contexts.

Chapter 14: BitFit: Binary Compression for Efficient Model Tuning

14.1 Introduction to BitFit

BitFit stands as a novel approach in the domain of machine learning, particularly focusing on optimizing model storage and efficiency through binary compression of model weights. This technique dramatically reduces the storage overhead required for AI models without significantly compromising their performance. Originating from research that seeks to address the growing concerns over the size of state-of-the-art models, BitFit provides an elegant solution for deploying advanced AI capabilities on devices with limited storage capacity or in environments where bandwidth for model updates is constrained.

14.2 Principles of BitFit

BitFit operates by applying a binary compression scheme to the weights of neural networks, effectively reducing the precision of these weights to binary or near-binary values. This process involves:

- Weight Quantization: Transforming continuous or high-precision weight values into binary or near-binary equivalents, significantly reducing the amount of storage needed.
- Fine-Tuning with Binary Constraints: Once weights are compressed, BitFit fine-tunes the model within this binary constraint, ensuring that the model can still learn and adapt to its task without the need for high-precision weights.
- Efficient Storage and Distribution: The resultant binary-compressed models require far less storage space and can be distributed more efficiently across networks, making updates faster and more feasible in bandwidth-limited scenarios.

14.3 Applications and Impact

The implications of BitFit are wide-ranging, with potential benefits across multiple areas:

- Edge Computing: Enables more sophisticated AI models to be deployed directly on edge devices, such as smartphones, IoT devices, and embedded systems, where storage space is at a premium.
- Model Deployment in Developing Regions: Facilitates the deployment of advanced AI solutions in areas with limited internet bandwidth, making it possible to bring AI-driven innovations to a broader audience.
- Sustainability: By reducing the size of models, BitFit contributes to lowering the environmental impact associated with data storage and transfer over the internet.

14.4 Challenges and Future Directions

While BitFit offers a promising avenue for model compression, it also introduces challenges, particularly in maintaining model accuracy and performance. The process of quantizing weights to binary values can lead to information loss, which in turn might affect the model's ability to accurately capture complex patterns in the data.

Future research in this area is likely to focus on developing more sophisticated quantization and fine-tuning algorithms that can minimize performance degradation. Additionally, there is ongoing work in exploring the application of BitFit and similar techniques across a wider range of model architectures and tasks, including those with inherently high complexity or those requiring high levels of precision.

In conclusion, BitFit represents a significant step forward in the quest to make AI models more accessible and sustainable. By addressing the critical challenge of model size and storage efficiency, BitFit opens up new possibilities for the deployment of AI technologies, particularly in resource-constrained environments, thereby broadening the reach and impact of AI across the globe.

Chapter 15: Adapters: Modular Fine-Tuning for Efficient Adaptation

15.1 Introduction to Adapters

Adapters present an innovative approach to fine-tuning pre-trained models for specific tasks without the need to extensively retrain the entire network. This method involves inserting small, trainable modules between the layers of an existing model. These modules are designed to adapt the model's internal representations to new tasks with minimal changes to the original model's weights. This approach offers a balance between the flexibility of full model fine-tuning and the efficiency of feature extraction methods, making it particularly attractive for applications where computational resources are limited or where preserving the integrity of the original model is important.

15.2 Principles of Adapter Modules

The core idea behind adapters is to introduce lightweight, task-specific layers into a pre-trained network. These layers, or adapter modules, are typically composed of a down-projection that reduces the dimensionality of the layer's input, a non-linear activation function, and an up-projection that restores the dimensionality to match the output of the original layer. By training only these adapter modules while keeping the pre-trained weights frozen, adapters enable rapid adaptation to new tasks with significantly reduced computational overhead.

15.3 Applications and Impact

Adapters have been successfully applied in various domains, demonstrating their versatility and effectiveness:

- Natural Language Processing (NLP): In tasks such as language translation, sentiment analysis, and text classification, adapters allow for the efficient customization of large language models like BERT or GPT to specific languages or domains without the need for extensive retraining.
- Computer Vision: Adapters enable the adaptation of pre-trained image recognition models to new tasks or datasets, such as identifying specific types of objects in images or adapting to different visual domains.
- Cross-Domain Transfer Learning: Adapters facilitate the transfer of knowledge across different domains or tasks by efficiently tuning pre-trained models to perform well on tasks for which they were not originally trained.

15.4 Challenges and Future Directions

One challenge in using adapters is designing the adapter architecture in a way that optimally balances task-specific adaptability with computational efficiency. Finding the right size and configuration for the adapter modules to achieve high performance without introducing significant overhead remains an area of ongoing research.

Future directions in the development of adapter methods include exploring more sophisticated architectures for the adapter modules, such as incorporating attention mechanisms or dynamic routing layers that can more effectively modulate the flow of information through the model based on the task at hand. Additionally, research into the combined use of adapters with other fine-tuning and model compression techniques could further enhance their efficiency and applicability across a broader range of tasks and models.

In conclusion, adapters offer a promising approach to the fine-tuning of pre-trained models, providing a practical solution for rapidly adapting large and complex models to new tasks with minimal computational cost. As this approach continues to evolve, it is poised to play a key role in making state-of-the-art AI models more accessible and adaptable, thereby accelerating innovation and application of AI across diverse domains.

Chapter 16: Sparsely Activated Modules (SAM): Enhancing Efficiency with Selective Training

16.1 Introduction to Sparsely Activated Modules (SAM)

Sparsely Activated Modules (SAM) introduce a paradigm shift in fine-tuning methodologies for deep learning models. This technique focuses on selectively training only a subset of the model's modules or layers during the fine-tuning process. By promoting sparsity in the activation and training of these modules, SAM aims to enhance computational efficiency and reduce the resources required for updating large-scale models. This approach is particularly relevant for scenarios where computational resources are constrained or when fine-tuning needs to be performed frequently and efficiently.

16.2 Principles of SAM

The underlying principle of SAM is to identify and activate only those parts of the model that are most relevant to the task at hand, while leaving the remainder of the model unchanged. This selective activation is achieved through mechanisms such as attention gating, where the model learns which modules are critical for a given input, or through pre-defined rules that determine module activation based on task-specific criteria.

The key components of SAM include:

- Sparse Activation: Dynamically selecting which modules within the network are activated during the forward pass, based on the relevance to the task.
- Efficient Training: Limiting the backpropagation of errors and the update of weights to only those modules that are activated, significantly reducing the computational load.
- Adaptability: The ability to apply SAM to different parts of the model and to various types of neural networks, enhancing its versatility across tasks and domains.

16.3 Applications and Impact

The applications of SAM are wide-ranging and demonstrate its potential to revolutionize model fine-tuning:

- Large-Scale Language Models: In NLP, SAM can be used to fine-tune massive language models more efficiently by activating only the relevant parts of the model for specific tasks such as translation, summarization, or sentiment analysis.
- Computer Vision: For image recognition or object detection tasks, SAM enables the selective training of model components that are most pertinent to recognizing specific classes or features, optimizing computational resources.

- Recommendation Systems: SAM can enhance the efficiency of fine-tuning recommendation algorithms by focusing on the components of the model that are most relevant to the user's current context or preferences.

16.4 Challenges and Future Directions

Implementing SAM poses challenges such as determining the optimal criteria for module activation and ensuring that the sparsity induced by selective training does not compromise the model's overall performance. Additionally, developing scalable and generalizable methods for identifying which modules to activate for a given task remains an area of active research.

Future directions include exploring adaptive mechanisms for module selection that can dynamically adjust based on the model's performance or the complexity of the task. Integrating SAM with other fine-tuning and model compression techniques could also yield synergies that further enhance efficiency and performance.

In conclusion, Sparsely Activated Modules represent a promising approach to making the fine-tuning of deep learning models more efficient and resource-effective. As this technique continues to develop, it holds the potential to significantly impact how models are updated and adapted, facilitating the rapid deployment of advanced AI capabilities across a broad spectrum of applications.

Chapter 17: HyperNetworks: Streamlining Fine-Tuning through Dynamic Weight Generation

17.1 Introduction to HyperNetworks

HyperNetworks embody a transformative approach within the domain of neural network optimization, where a secondary, smaller neural network, termed the HyperNetwork, is employed to generate the weights for a larger, primary network. This innovative method offers a pathway to significantly reduce the computational overhead associated with the fine-tuning of large models, by dynamically adjusting the parameters of the target network in a context-sensitive manner.

17.2 Conceptual Framework of HyperNetworks

At the core of HyperNetworks lies the principle of parameter generation. Instead of directly learning and updating a vast number of weights within the primary network, HyperNetworks streamline this process by learning to produce these weights based on the task at hand. This method not only reduces the number of parameters that need to be directly optimized but also introduces a level of flexibility and adaptability that is unparalleled in traditional fine-tuning approaches.

Key features of HyperNetworks include:

- Dynamic Weight Generation: The ability to produce weights for the primary network on-the-fly, allowing for rapid adaptation to new tasks or data.
- Reduced Parameter Space: By concentrating the learning process within the smaller HyperNetwork, the overall parameter space that requires optimization is significantly diminished.
- Context-Sensitive Adaptation: HyperNetworks can generate different weights for the primary network depending on the input, making the model highly adaptable to varying contexts or tasks.

17.3 Applications and Benefits

HyperNetworks find utility in a variety of applications across machine learning:

- Efficient Fine-Tuning of Large Models: In scenarios where the computational cost of fine-tuning large models is prohibitive, HyperNetworks offer a more efficient alternative by reducing the number of parameters that need direct optimization.
- Task-Specific Model Adaptation: For multi-task learning or transfer learning, HyperNetworks can dynamically adjust the primary network to better suit specific tasks, improving performance without extensive retraining.

- Model Personalization: In personalized AI applications, such as user-specific recommendation systems or adaptive learning platforms, HyperNetworks enable the model to tailor its behavior to individual users by generating user-specific weights.

17.4 Challenges and Research Directions

While HyperNetworks present a promising avenue for model optimization, several challenges remain:

- Design Complexity: The design and training of the HyperNetwork itself can be complex, requiring careful consideration to ensure that it effectively captures the necessary dynamics for weight generation.
- Generalization: Ensuring that the HyperNetwork generalizes well across different tasks and inputs is crucial to its success, necessitating ongoing research into architecture and training methods.
- Integration with Existing Models: Integrating HyperNetworks with existing neural network architectures in a way that maximizes their potential while maintaining model performance is an area of active exploration.

17.5 Future Perspectives

The future of HyperNetworks in fine-tuning and model optimization is bright, with ongoing research aimed at enhancing their efficiency, adaptability, and ease of integration. Innovations in architecture design, training algorithms, and applications are likely to further cement the role of HyperNetworks in creating more dynamic, efficient, and task-adaptive neural networks.

In conclusion, HyperNetworks represent a cutting-edge approach to fine-tuning and model optimization, offering a pathway to significantly reduce the computational burden while increasing the adaptability of neural networks. As this field evolves, HyperNetworks are poised to play a pivotal role in the next generation of machine learning systems, enabling more flexible, efficient, and personalized AI solutions.

Chapter 18: Patient Knowledge Distillation (PKD): Enhancing Model Efficiency through Iterative Learning

18.1 Introduction to Patient Knowledge Distillation

Patient Knowledge Distillation (PKD) represents an advanced fine-tuning methodology that leverages the concept of knowledge distillation in a novel, iterative manner. Unlike conventional distillation processes, PKD involves multiple stages of fine-tuning, where the model, once fine-tuned, serves as a 'teacher' for the subsequent fine-tuning steps. This approach facilitates a more gradual and nuanced transfer of knowledge from the teacher model to the student model, effectively enhancing the learning efficiency and overall performance of the fine-tuned model.

18.2 The PKD Process

The foundational principle of PKD lies in its iterative nature, which allows for a step-wise refinement and consolidation of knowledge within the model. This process can be broken down into several key phases:

- Initial Model Training: The base model is first trained on a general dataset to learn a broad range of features and capabilities.
- First Iteration of Fine-Tuning: The model is then fine-tuned on a more specific dataset or task, adjusting its parameters to better suit the specialized requirements.
- Distillation to a New Model: The fine-tuned model now acts as a teacher, imparting its learned knowledge to a new, often smaller, student model through the distillation process.
- Iterative Refinement: This cycle of fine-tuning and distillation is repeated, with each iteration refining the student model's performance and knowledge base.

18.3 Advantages of PKD

PKD offers several distinct advantages over traditional fine-tuning and distillation methods:

- Enhanced Learning Efficiency: By iteratively refining the model, PKD promotes a more efficient consolidation of knowledge, leading to improved model performance with potentially fewer training cycles.
- Gradual Knowledge Transfer: The gradual transfer of knowledge allows the student model to assimilate complex information in a more manageable manner, enhancing its ability to generalize from the teacher model's insights.
- Resource Optimization: PKD can lead to the development of smaller, more efficient models that retain the performance characteristics of their larger counterparts, optimizing computational resources.

18.4 Applications and Case Studies

PKD has found applications across a variety of domains, including:

- Language Processing: In natural language processing tasks, PKD can help in refining language models for specific linguistic styles or domains.
- Image Recognition: For image recognition, PKD can assist in tailoring models to recognize particular types of visual data with greater accuracy.
- Personalized AI: In personalized AI applications, PKD can be used to adapt models to individual user behaviors and preferences over time.

18.5 Challenges and Future Directions

While PKD offers significant benefits, it also presents challenges, such as:

- Complexity in Iterative Training: Managing the iterative distillation process requires careful planning to ensure that each cycle contributes positively to the model's development.
- Balancing Generalization and Specialization: Finding the right balance between retaining the general capabilities of the teacher model and specializing the student model is critical for success.
- Optimizing Resource Use: Ensuring that the iterative process does not lead to excessive computational demands is essential for the practical application of PKD.

18.6 Conclusion

Patient Knowledge Distillation stands as a promising approach in the fine-tuning of machine learning models, offering a nuanced method for enhancing model performance through iterative learning and distillation. As the field progresses, further research into optimizing the PKD process, exploring its applications in various domains, and addressing its challenges will undoubtedly expand its utility and effectiveness in creating sophisticated, efficient AI systems.

Chapter 19: Data-Free Knowledge Distillation: Synthetic Data for Model Refinement

19.1 Introduction to Data-Free Knowledge Distillation

Data-Free Knowledge Distillation (DFKD) is an innovative approach in the field of machine learning that addresses the challenge of fine-tuning models when access to the original training data is restricted or unavailable. This technique involves generating synthetic data that imitates the properties of the original dataset, based on the knowledge encapsulated within a pre-trained model. DFKD enables the distillation and refinement of models without direct reliance on the original data, ensuring privacy, security, and compliance with data usage regulations.

19.2 Generating Synthetic Data for Distillation

The process of DFKD hinges on the ability to create synthetic data that effectively captures the essence of the original training dataset. This involves:

- Model Inversion: Leveraging the pre-trained model to infer input features that would lead to specific outputs, essentially working backwards from the model's predictions to generate input data.
- Feature Mimicry: Employing techniques to mimic the statistical properties of the original dataset, ensuring that the synthetic data retains the essential characteristics necessary for effective learning.
- Optimization Techniques: Utilizing optimization algorithms to refine the synthetic data generation process, maximizing the fidelity of the generated data to the original dataset's distribution.

19.3 Applications and Impact

DFKD has significant implications across various domains, particularly in scenarios where data privacy or availability is a concern:

- Privacy-sensitive Sectors: In industries such as healthcare and finance, where data privacy regulations restrict the sharing of sensitive information, DFKD allows for model refinement without compromising data security.
- Model Compression: DFKD can facilitate the compression of large models into more efficient formats by fine-tuning them on synthetic data, enabling their deployment on resource-constrained devices.
- Transfer Learning: When adapting models to new tasks for which specific training data is scarce or unavailable, DFKD provides a method for generating relevant synthetic data to facilitate the transfer learning process.

19.4 Challenges and Future Directions

While DFKD offers a promising solution to data availability and privacy issues, it also presents several challenges:

- Synthetic Data Quality: Ensuring that the synthetic data adequately represents the complexity and diversity of the original dataset is crucial for maintaining model performance.
- Model Bias: There is a risk that synthetic data may introduce or exacerbate biases within the model, necessitating careful monitoring and adjustment of the data generation process.
- Computational Efficiency: The process of generating high-quality synthetic data can be computationally intensive, requiring optimization to make DFKD practical for large-scale applications.

Future research in DFKD is likely to focus on improving the efficiency and effectiveness of synthetic data generation, exploring new applications for the technique, and addressing ethical considerations related to model training on synthetic versus real data.

19.5 Conclusion

Data-Free Knowledge Distillation represents a groundbreaking approach to overcoming the challenges associated with data privacy and availability in machine learning. By enabling the generation of synthetic data for fine-tuning and distillation, DFKD opens up new possibilities for model development and refinement across a wide range of applications. As the field advances, DFKD is poised to play a critical role in the evolution of machine learning, offering a versatile and privacy-conscious solution for training and refining AI models.

Chapter 20: Prefix Tuning: Enhancing Model Adaptability with Trainable Prefixes

20.1 The Concept of Prefix Tuning

Prefix Tuning is a novel fine-tuning approach designed to enhance the adaptability of large language models to specific tasks with minimal changes to their underlying architecture. This method involves the addition of trainable vectors, known as prefixes, to the input sequences of a model. These prefixes serve as task-specific adjustments, guiding the model's attention mechanism and processing pathways to better align with the desired outputs. Originating from the idea that small, targeted modifications can significantly influence a model's behavior, Prefix Tuning offers a flexible and efficient alternative to traditional fine-tuning methods.

20.2 Mechanism and Implementation

At its core, Prefix Tuning operates by prepending a set of trainable parameters to the input sequences before they are processed by the model. These parameters are optimized during a targeted training phase, where the model learns to associate specific prefix patterns with task-relevant processing strategies. Key aspects include:

- Prefix Design: The design of prefixes, including their length and structure, is critical for balancing model performance with computational efficiency.
- Training Process: During training, the prefixes are adjusted through backpropagation based on their impact on model output, allowing them to effectively encapsulate task-specific knowledge.
- Integration with Existing Architectures: Prefix Tuning can be applied to a wide range of model architectures without requiring significant modifications, making it a versatile tool for model adaptation.

20.3 Advantages Over Traditional Models

Prefix Tuning presents several advantages over conventional fine-tuning approaches:

- Efficiency: By adjusting only a small set of parameters, Prefix Tuning requires significantly less computational resources, making it ideal for applications with limited processing power.
- Flexibility: The method allows for rapid adaptation to new tasks without the need to retrain the entire model, facilitating quicker deployment of customized solutions.
- Task-Specific Adaptation: The use of task-specific prefixes enables models to maintain high performance across a diverse set of tasks, even when they significantly differ from the model's original training data.

20.4 Use Cases and Applications

The versatility of Prefix Tuning has led to its successful application in a variety of domains, including:

- Natural Language Processing (NLP): Enhancing performance on specific NLP tasks such as translation, summarization, and sentiment analysis.
- Personalized Content Generation: Customizing AI-generated content to align with specific styles or themes by training task-specific prefixes.
- Domain-Specific Adaptations: Quickly adapting models to specialized fields, such as legal or medical texts, where domain knowledge is crucial.

20.5 Challenges and Future Directions

While Prefix Tuning offers a promising avenue for efficient model adaptation, it also presents challenges that merit further investigation:

- Optimal Prefix Design: Determining the most effective prefix configurations for various tasks remains an area of active research.
- Transferability Across Models: Exploring the extent to which prefixes trained for one model can be effectively transferred to another.
- Scalability: Assessing the scalability of Prefix Tuning for extremely large models and datasets.

Future developments in Prefix Tuning are likely to focus on enhancing its effectiveness and applicability across a broader range of tasks and models. As the technique matures, it has the potential to significantly impact the field of machine learning by providing a more adaptable and resource-efficient method for model fine-tuning.

20.6 Conclusion

Prefix Tuning represents a significant advancement in the fine-tuning of machine learning models, offering a balance between adaptability, efficiency, and performance. By enabling models to be quickly customized for a wide range of tasks with minimal computational overhead, Prefix Tuning paves the way for more versatile and accessible AI applications. As research continues to refine and expand the capabilities of this approach, Prefix Tuning is poised to become a cornerstone technique in the development of task-specific AI solutions.

Chapter 21: Continual Fine-Tuning: Combatting Catastrophic Forgetting in Sequential Task Learning

21.1 Introduction to Catastrophic Forgetting

Catastrophic forgetting is a significant challenge in machine learning, particularly in neural networks. It occurs when a model, after being trained on a sequence of tasks, retains knowledge from the most recent task at the expense of previously learned information. This phenomenon undermines the model's ability to perform well across a series of tasks, which is crucial for applications requiring versatility and adaptability. Continual fine-tuning methods aim to address this issue by enabling models to retain knowledge across a wide range of tasks without significant performance degradation on older tasks.

21.2 Strategies for Continual Fine-Tuning

To mitigate catastrophic forgetting, several strategies have been developed, each with its unique approach to preserving previously acquired knowledge while incorporating new information:

- Elastic Weight Consolidation (EWC): EWC applies a regularization term that discourages significant changes to weights important for previous tasks, thus balancing the need to learn new tasks with the preservation of old knowledge.
- Replay Mechanisms: These involve retaining a subset of data from previous tasks and interleaving it with new task data during training, simulating a continuous learning environment.
- Progressive Neural Networks: This approach involves adding new neural network components for each task while keeping the existing network structure fixed and transferring knowledge via lateral connections.

21.3 Implementation Challenges

Implementing continual fine-tuning effectively presents several challenges:

- Memory Management: Efficiently managing memory to store relevant data from previous tasks without overwhelming the system.
- Task Interference: Minimizing interference between tasks, where learning one task negatively impacts the performance on another.
- Scalability: Ensuring the method scales well with an increasing number of tasks without compromising model performance or efficiency.

21.4 Advantages of Continual Fine-Tuning

The adoption of continual fine-tuning techniques offers several advantages:

- Versatility: Models become capable of learning new tasks without forgetting previous ones, increasing their applicability across various domains.
- Efficiency: Reduces the need for retraining from scratch for every new task, saving computational resources and time.
- Dynamic Adaptation: Enables models to adapt dynamically to new information or tasks in environments where data is continually evolving.

21.5 Use Cases and Applications

Continual fine-tuning has broad applicability across many areas, including:

- Autonomous Systems: For systems that operate in changing environments and need to adapt to new scenarios without losing prior knowledge.
- Personalized Learning: In applications where models need to continually adapt to individual user preferences or behaviors over time.
- Multi-Domain Operations: For models operating across multiple domains or tasks, maintaining high performance across all areas.

21.6 Future Directions

The field of continual learning is ripe with opportunities for innovation, particularly in developing more efficient strategies to manage the trade-off between learning new tasks and preserving knowledge from previous ones. Research is likely to focus on creating more sophisticated architectures and algorithms that can dynamically adjust to the demands of continual learning, possibly incorporating advances in neuroscience and cognitive science to mimic human-like learning patterns more closely.

21.7 Conclusion

Continual fine-tuning represents a pivotal advancement in machine learning, addressing the critical challenge of catastrophic forgetting. By enabling models to maintain performance across a sequence of tasks, continual fine-tuning not only enhances the versatility and effectiveness of AI systems but also brings us closer to achieving true artificial general intelligence. As research in this area progresses, we can anticipate the development of even more sophisticated models capable of seamless, lifelong learning.

Chapter 22: Patient Knowledge Distillation (PKD): Enhancing Model Performance through Iterative Refinement

22.1 Introduction to Knowledge Distillation

Knowledge Distillation (KD) is a technique in machine learning where knowledge is transferred from a larger, more complex model (teacher) to a smaller, simpler model (student). The goal is to improve the performance of the student model by leveraging the insights and complexities captured by the teacher model. Patient Knowledge Distillation (PKD) extends this concept by introducing an iterative distillation process, where the student model undergoes multiple rounds of training, gradually absorbing more nuanced knowledge from the teacher.

22.2 The PKD Process

PKD involves several key steps that differentiate it from traditional KD:

- Initial Distillation: Similar to standard KD, the process begins with the student model learning from the teacher model's outputs. This step establishes a baseline performance for the student model.
- Iterative Refinement: Unlike traditional KD, PKD involves multiple rounds of distillation. After the initial phase, the student model's performance is evaluated, and areas for improvement are identified.
- Role Reversal: In PKD, the roles of teacher and student can dynamically change. Once the student model achieves a certain level of performance, it can become the teacher for the next iteration, further refining its knowledge or teaching another student model.
- Patient Evaluation: Throughout the PKD process, patience is key. Each iteration is carefully monitored to ensure that genuine learning occurs, avoiding overfitting or the diminishing returns of excessive iterations.

22.3 Advantages of PKD

PKD offers several advantages over traditional KD and other machine learning methodologies:

- Efficiency: By refining the student model iteratively, PKD can achieve higher performance levels without the need for larger, more complex models.
- Flexibility: The iterative nature of PKD allows for adjustments in the teaching process, making it adaptable to the student model's specific needs and learning capabilities.
- Scalability: PKD is scalable to various domains and applications, from natural language processing to image recognition, enhancing the versatility of machine learning models.

22.4 Applications and Use Cases

PKD has been successfully applied in numerous areas, demonstrating its versatility and effectiveness:

- Model Compression: Reducing the size of large models while retaining their performance, making them suitable for deployment on devices with limited computational resources.
- Performance Boosting: Enhancing the accuracy and efficiency of smaller models for tasks where deploying large models is impractical.
- Continuous Learning: Facilitating the process of lifelong learning in models by allowing them to iteratively refine their knowledge over time.

22.5 Challenges and Future Directions

Despite its advantages, PKD faces several challenges:

- Optimization: Determining the optimal number of iterations and the criteria for role reversal between teacher and student models.
- Generalization: Ensuring that models trained via PKD generalize well to unseen data and real-world scenarios.
- Complexity Management: Managing the increased complexity and computational cost associated with multiple rounds of distillation.

The future of PKD lies in addressing these challenges and exploring new applications. Research is likely to focus on optimizing the PKD process, developing more efficient algorithms for iteration and evaluation, and applying PKD to a broader range of tasks and domains.

22.6 Conclusion

Patient Knowledge Distillation represents a significant advancement in the field of machine learning, offering a method to enhance model performance through careful, iterative refinement. By combining the strengths of knowledge distillation with a patient, iterative approach, PKD opens new avenues for developing highly efficient and effective models capable of tackling complex tasks with improved accuracy and efficiency. As the field progresses, PKD is poised to play a crucial role in the continued evolution of artificial intelligence.

Chapter 23: Data-Free Knowledge Distillation: Unlocking Model Potential Without Original Data

23.1 Overview of Knowledge Distillation

Knowledge Distillation (KD) is a technique that involves transferring knowledge from a larger, more complex model (teacher) to a smaller, more efficient model (student). Traditionally, KD relies on the original training data to facilitate this transfer. However, in many real-world scenarios, the original dataset might not be available due to privacy concerns, data loss, or regulatory restrictions. Data-Free Knowledge Distillation (DFKD) emerges as a solution to this challenge, enabling the distillation process without access to the original training data.

23.2 The Essence of Data-Free Knowledge Distillation

DFKD leverages synthetic data generated from the teacher model itself or through other means to train the student model. The process involves several key components:

- Synthetic Data Generation: Techniques are employed to generate new data samples that mimic the distribution of the original dataset. This can involve using the teacher model's outputs, inputs, or both to create data that captures the underlying data distribution.
- Teacher-Student Training: The student model learns from the synthetic data under the guidance of the teacher model. The training objective is to minimize the difference in outputs between the student and teacher models, thereby transferring the knowledge.
- Adaptation Techniques: Various strategies are employed to ensure that the synthetic data is effective for training the student model. These can include regularization techniques, noise addition, and optimization algorithms designed to make the synthetic data more representative of real-world scenarios.

23.3 Advantages of DFKD

DFKD offers several significant benefits:

- Privacy Preservation: Enables knowledge transfer without needing access to sensitive or proprietary data, adhering to privacy regulations.
- Accessibility: Facilitates the use of KD techniques in situations where the original dataset is lost or inaccessible.
- Efficiency: Reduces the dependency on large datasets for training, potentially lowering the computational cost and time required for the distillation process.

23.4 Applications and Use Cases

DFKD has been applied in various domains with promising results:

- Model Compression: Allowing for the compression of models in data-sensitive environments without sacrificing significant performance.
- Cross-Domain Adaptation: Enabling the transfer of knowledge from a model trained in one domain to another domain where data may not be readily available.
- Enhancing Privacy: Useful in scenarios where data cannot be shared between entities, allowing for model improvement without data exchange.

23.5 Challenges and Future Directions

Despite its advantages, DFKD faces challenges:

- Quality of Synthetic Data: Generating synthetic data that is representative enough to effectively train the student model remains a significant challenge.
- Evaluation Metrics: Assessing the effectiveness of DFKD and the quality of the generated data without the original dataset for benchmarking.
- Domain-Specific Limitations: The effectiveness of DFKD can vary significantly across different domains, necessitating further research into domain-specific adaptation techniques.

Future research in DFKD is likely to focus on improving synthetic data generation techniques, developing more robust evaluation metrics, and exploring new applications in privacy-sensitive environments.

23.6 Conclusion

Data-Free Knowledge Distillation represents a groundbreaking approach to knowledge transfer in machine learning, especially in contexts where data privacy, accessibility, or availability are of concern. By enabling the distillation process without the original training data, DFKD opens up new possibilities for model improvement and adaptation across a wide range of applications. As the field progresses, refining synthetic data generation methods and overcoming current limitations will be key to unlocking the full potential of DFKD in the broader landscape of artificial intelligence development.

Open-Source Tools and Libraries

Chapter 24: Axolotl: A Flexible Framework for Fine-Tuning Across Architectures

24.1 Introduction to Axolotl

Axolotl represents a significant advancement in the field of machine learning fine-tuning, offering a versatile and open-source platform that supports multiple configurations and architectures. This framework is designed to streamline and enhance the process of fine-tuning machine learning models across various tasks, making it accessible for researchers and practitioners alike. By providing a unified interface for fine-tuning, Axolotl facilitates experimentation with different models and fine-tuning strategies, fostering innovation and efficiency in AI model development.

24.2 Key Features and Capabilities

- Multi-Architecture Support: Axolotl is built to accommodate a wide range of model architectures, from conventional neural networks to state-of-the-art transformer models, ensuring broad applicability across different AI domains.
- Configurable Fine-Tuning Strategies: The framework allows for the customization of fine-tuning parameters and strategies, enabling users to tailor the process to their specific needs and objectives. This includes adjustments to learning rates, optimization algorithms, and training schedules.
- Plug-and-Play Components: With its modular design, Axolotl enables easy integration of new models, data processing pipelines, and fine-tuning techniques, encouraging experimentation and rapid prototyping.

24.3 Advantages Over Traditional Fine-Tuning Methods

Axolotl stands out for its flexibility and user-friendly design, offering several advantages:

- Efficiency: By streamlining the fine-tuning process, Axolotl reduces the time and computational resources required to optimize models for specific tasks.
- Experimentation: The framework's configurability and support for multiple architectures make it an ideal platform for exploring new fine-tuning approaches and model combinations.
- Accessibility: Axolotl lowers the barrier to entry for fine-tuning advanced models, making cutting-edge AI technology more accessible to a broader audience.

24.4 Use Cases and Applications

Axolotl's versatility makes it suitable for a wide range of applications, including but not limited to:

- Natural Language Processing (NLP): Fine-tuning language models for tasks such as sentiment analysis, machine translation, and text summarization.

- Computer Vision: Optimizing image recognition and object detection models for specific domains or datasets.
- Reinforcement Learning: Adjusting policy networks for more efficient learning in simulated environments.

24.5 Challenges and Opportunities

While Axolotl offers a promising platform for fine-tuning, there are challenges to consider:

- Complexity Management: Ensuring that the framework remains user-friendly as it expands to support more architectures and configurations.
- Performance Optimization: Balancing the flexibility of the framework with the need for efficient processing and low-latency model training.

The future development of Axolotl involves addressing these challenges while expanding its capabilities, including the integration of more advanced AI models and the exploration of novel fine-tuning methodologies.

24.6 Conclusion

Axolotl represents a forward-thinking approach to fine-tuning in machine learning, providing a flexible, efficient, and accessible framework for enhancing model performance across a variety of tasks and domains. As the AI field continues to evolve, tools like Axolotl play a crucial role in enabling researchers and practitioners to push the boundaries of what's possible with machine learning, driving innovation and progress in artificial intelligence.

Chapter 25: AdapterHub: Streamlining Adapter-Based Fine-Tuning

25.1 Introduction to AdapterHub

AdapterHub is a groundbreaking platform designed to facilitate adapter-based fine-tuning in machine learning. As a central repository of pre-trained adapter modules, it simplifies the process of fine-tuning across a wide array of models, making it an invaluable resource for researchers and developers seeking to leverage the power of adapters for task-specific model optimization.

25.2 Core Features of AdapterHub

- Comprehensive Repository: AdapterHub hosts a wide variety of adapter modules pre-trained on diverse datasets and tasks, offering a rich resource for users to find the perfect fit for their specific needs.
- Cross-Model Compatibility: The platform supports a range of model architectures, enabling seamless integration of adapter modules into existing machine learning pipelines without significant modifications.
- Community-Driven: AdapterHub encourages contributions from the AI research community, continuously expanding its collection of adapter modules through user submissions and collaborations.

25.3 Advantages of Using AdapterHub

AdapterHub offers several key benefits over traditional fine-tuning approaches:

- Efficiency: By providing access to pre-trained adapter modules, AdapterHub significantly reduces the computational resources and time required for fine-tuning models on new tasks.
- Flexibility: The platform's support for various model architectures and its extensive repository of adapters make it a versatile tool for a wide range of applications in machine learning.
- Ease of Use: AdapterHub's user-friendly interface and integration capabilities allow for straightforward implementation of adapter-based fine-tuning, lowering the barrier to entry for advanced model optimization techniques.

25.4 Applications and Success Stories

The utility of AdapterHub spans multiple domains, including but not limited to:

- Natural Language Processing: Enhancing performance on tasks such as text classification, language generation, and sentiment analysis.
- Computer Vision: Improving accuracy in image recognition, object detection, and visual question answering.
- Voice and Audio Processing: Optimizing models for speech recognition, audio classification, and sound generation.

25.5 Overcoming Challenges and Future Directions

While AdapterHub has made adapter-based fine-tuning more accessible, there are still challenges to address:

- Integration with Emerging Models: Keeping pace with the rapid development of new model architectures and ensuring compatibility with the latest advancements in AI.
- Quality Control: Ensuring the high quality of adapters available on the platform, including robust evaluation and validation mechanisms.

Future developments for AdapterHub may focus on expanding its repository to include adapters for cutting-edge models, enhancing platform functionalities to support more complex fine-tuning workflows, and fostering a larger, more active community of contributors.

25.6 Conclusion

AdapterHub represents a significant advancement in the landscape of machine learning fine-tuning, providing a centralized, accessible, and efficient solution for implementing adapter-based approaches. By streamlining the process of optimizing models for specific tasks, AdapterHub not only enhances model performance but also accelerates the pace of innovation in AI research and application. As the platform continues to evolve, it will undoubtedly play a pivotal role in shaping the future of machine learning fine-tuning strategies.

Chapter 26: LoRA Library: Simplifying LoRA Fine-Tuning

26.1 Introduction to LoRA Library

The LoRA Library, hosted on GitHub by Microsoft, is a specialized tool designed to streamline the implementation of Low-Rank Adaptation (LoRA) fine-tuning techniques. LoRA represents a powerful method for adapting large pre-trained models to new tasks with minimal computational overhead, and the LoRA Library aims to make this technology more accessible to the broader AI research and development community.

26.2 Key Features of the LoRA Library

- Comprehensive Documentation: The library provides detailed instructions for implementing LoRA fine-tuning, including step-by-step guides, best practices, and troubleshooting tips.
- Wide Model Support: It supports a range of pre-trained models, offering flexibility for researchers and practitioners looking to apply LoRA across different architectures and domains.
- Community Contributions: Encourages contributions from users, facilitating the sharing of improvements, new features, and model extensions within the community.

26.3 Benefits of Using the LoRA Library

The LoRA Library offers several advantages:

- Efficiency: By focusing on low-rank matrix adaptations, it allows for efficient fine-tuning of large models without the need for extensive computational resources.
- Simplicity: The library simplifies the process of applying LoRA, making it accessible to users without in-depth expertise in model fine-tuning.
- Flexibility: It provides the means to fine-tune models on a wide variety of tasks and datasets, enhancing model performance across numerous applications.

26.4 Applications and Case Studies

Applications of the LoRA Library span multiple areas, such as:

- Natural Language Processing (NLP): Fine-tuning language models for improved performance on tasks like translation, summarization, and question-answering.
- Computer Vision: Adapting vision models for enhanced object detection, image classification, and facial recognition capabilities.
- Custom Applications: Facilitating research and development in niche areas by allowing for the rapid adaptation of models to specialized tasks.

26.5 Addressing Challenges and Future Prospects

Challenges and potential areas for future development include:

- Scalability: Ensuring the library scales efficiently with the growing size and complexity of state-of-the-art models.
- User Experience: Continuously improving the documentation and usability of the library to accommodate a broader range of users.
- Community Engagement: Encouraging more community involvement for a diverse range of contributions, including novel applications, model support, and feature enhancements.

26.6 Conclusion

The LoRA Library by Microsoft represents a significant step forward in democratizing the application of advanced fine-tuning techniques like LoRA. By providing a user-friendly platform with comprehensive support and documentation, it opens up new possibilities for enhancing the performance of pre-trained models across a broad spectrum of tasks and domains. As the library evolves, it is poised to become an essential tool for AI researchers and practitioners looking to push the boundaries of what's possible with machine learning models.

Chapter 27: Easy Fine Tuner: Democratizing Fine-Tuning for All

27.1 Introduction to Easy Fine Tuner

Easy Fine Tuner stands as a beacon in the world of artificial intelligence, particularly in the realm of model fine-tuning. It is designed with the express purpose of making the fine-tuning of machine learning models accessible to a broader audience, including those without a deep technical background in AI. This platform provides a user-friendly interface that simplifies the complexity involved in adjusting pre-trained models for specific tasks.

27.2 Simplifying Fine-Tuning with a User-Friendly Interface

- Intuitive Design: Easy Fine Tuner features an intuitive, graphical user interface (GUI) that guides users through the fine-tuning process step by step, making it less daunting for beginners and non-technical users.
- Multiple Fine-Tuning Methods: It supports a variety of fine-tuning techniques, from traditional methods to more recent advancements, allowing users to experiment with different approaches to find the best fit for their specific needs.
- Automated Suggestions: The platform offers recommendations on fine-tuning parameters and methods based on the user's task and data, helping to optimize model performance without requiring deep expertise.

27.3 Advantages of Using Easy Fine Tuner

The key benefits of Easy Fine Tuner include:

- Accessibility: It lowers the barrier to entry for fine-tuning advanced machine learning models, opening up new possibilities for individuals and organizations lacking AI expertise.
- Flexibility: Users can fine-tune models for a wide range of applications, from text analysis and sentiment detection to image recognition and beyond.
- Efficiency: By streamlining the fine-tuning process, Easy Fine Tuner saves time and resources, enabling users to achieve optimal results with minimal effort.

27.4 Applications and Success Stories

Easy Fine Tuner has been successfully applied in various domains, such as:

- Education: Teachers and students use it for projects and research, applying AI to analyze educational data or create personalized learning experiences.
- Small Businesses: Non-technical entrepreneurs fine-tune models to analyze customer feedback, forecast trends, or automate routine tasks, enhancing their competitive edge.
- Non-Profits: Organizations leverage it to gain insights from data, supporting their missions with improved decision-making and operational efficiency.

27.5 Overcoming Challenges and Looking Ahead

While Easy Fine Tuner has made significant strides in democratizing AI, it faces challenges and opportunities for growth:

- Continual Improvement: Ongoing development is needed to keep the platform up-to-date with the latest fine-tuning techniques and user interface best practices.
- Education and Support: Expanding educational resources and support mechanisms can help users more effectively leverage the platform's capabilities.
- Community Engagement: Fostering a community of users and contributors can drive innovation and ensure the platform remains responsive to the evolving needs of its diverse user base.

27.6 Conclusion

Easy Fine Tuner represents a pivotal development in making the power of machine learning accessible to a wider audience. By providing a straightforward and versatile platform for fine-tuning AI models, it empowers users across various fields to harness the potential of AI for their specific needs. As the platform continues to evolve, it promises to play a crucial role in the democratization of AI technology, enabling more people and organizations to innovate and solve complex problems with the help of advanced machine learning.

Chapter 28: Hugging Face Datasets: Accelerating AI Research with Accessible Data

28.1 Introduction to Hugging Face Datasets

Hugging Face Datasets is a revolutionary library that provides the machine learning community with quick and easy access to a vast array of datasets. This initiative is part of Hugging Face's broader mission to democratize artificial intelligence by offering tools, data, and community support. The library covers a wide range of domains, including natural language processing (NLP), computer vision, and audio processing, facilitating research and development across diverse AI applications.

28.2 Key Features and Capabilities

- Diverse Collection: The library hosts thousands of datasets across various languages and domains, supporting a multitude of tasks such as text classification, question answering, translation, and more.
- Easy Access and Integration: With just a few lines of code, researchers and developers can download and prepare datasets for training machine learning models, streamlining the data preparation process.
- Community-Driven: Hugging Face Datasets is open-source and community-powered. Researchers, developers, and organizations contribute datasets, which undergo a review process to ensure quality and usability.

28.3 Advantages of Using Hugging Face Datasets

The primary benefits of the Hugging Face Datasets library include:

- Efficiency: Significantly reduces the time and effort required to access and preprocess data, allowing researchers and developers to focus more on model development and experimentation.
- Reproducibility: By providing standardized datasets, the library facilitates reproducible research, enabling the community to benchmark models accurately and consistently.
- Scalability: Supports loading datasets in a streaming manner, making it possible to work with very large datasets that cannot fit into memory, which is crucial for training sophisticated models.

28.4 Applications and Impact

Hugging Face Datasets has empowered a wide range of projects and research initiatives:

- Academic Research: Scholars utilize the library to access a broad spectrum of datasets for conducting cutting-edge research in NLP, computer vision, and more.

- Industry Innovations: Companies leverage these datasets to develop and refine AI models for real-world applications, such as language translation services, content moderation tools, and customer sentiment analysis.
- Community Projects: Open-source contributors and hobbyists experiment with diverse datasets to build innovative applications and contribute back to the community by sharing their findings and models.

28.5 Challenges and Future Directions

While Hugging Face Datasets has made significant contributions to the AI field, it continues to face challenges and opportunities for growth:

- Dataset Diversity: Ensuring a balanced representation of languages and domains remains a challenge, necessitating ongoing efforts to broaden the library's inclusivity.
- Quality Assurance: With the ever-growing number of datasets, maintaining high standards of quality and reliability requires continuous community engagement and automated validation mechanisms.
- Ethical Considerations: As with any data-centric initiative, addressing ethical concerns related to privacy, consent, and bias in datasets is crucial for fostering responsible AI development.

28.6 Conclusion

Hugging Face Datasets represents a pivotal resource in the AI ecosystem, providing unparalleled access to a wealth of data that accelerates innovation and research. By lowering barriers to data access and fostering a collaborative community, it plays a crucial role in the democratization of AI. Looking forward, Hugging Face Datasets is set to continue evolving, addressing challenges and expanding its offerings to support the next generation of AI advancements.

Fine Tuning Requirements

Chapter 29: Hardware Requirements for Fine-Tuning AI Models

Introduction

Fine-tuning pre-trained models is a common practice in machine learning to adapt a general model to a specific task. The computational resources required for fine-tuning vary significantly based on the model size, the complexity of the task, and the desired performance. This section provides guidelines on the minimum and recommended hardware specifications for fine-tuning various model sizes, explaining the impact on performance, cost, and efficiency.

Model Sizes and Scenarios

1. Small Models (e.g., BERT-base, DistilBERT)
   - Minimum Requirements: A single GPU with at least 8GB of VRAM (e.g., NVIDIA GTX 1080) can be sufficient for fine-tuning small models on modest datasets.
   - Recommended Setup: A GPU with 16GB of VRAM (e.g., NVIDIA Tesla T4 or A100) or multiple GPUs can significantly reduce training time and allow for more extensive hyperparameter tuning.
   - Performance Impact: Upgrading from the minimum to the recommended setup can decrease training times from days to hours, enabling more experiments and faster iterations.

2. Medium Models (e.g., BERT-large, RoBERTa-large)
   - Minimum Requirements: At least one GPU with 16GB of VRAM (e.g., NVIDIA Tesla T4 or A100).
   - Recommended Setup: Multiple GPUs with 32GB of VRAM each (e.g., NVIDIA Tesla V100 or A100) or a high-end GPU cluster.
   - Performance Impact: Using multiple GPUs can halve the training time and improve model performance through more effective parallel processing and data handling.

3. Large Models (e.g., GPT-3, T5-large)
   - Minimum Requirements: This is challenging due to the size of these models; however, accessing through cloud services with at least 48GB of VRAM per GPU (e.g., NVIDIA Tesla V100) could be considered a baseline.
   - Recommended Setup: A dedicated AI cluster with multiple high-end GPUs (e.g., NVIDIA A100s with 80GB of VRAM) or specialized hardware through cloud providers.
   - Performance Impact: The recommended setup can significantly reduce training times from weeks to days and allow for fine-tuning on larger datasets, improving model accuracy and generalization.

Factors to Consider

- Dataset Size: Larger datasets require more memory and processing power for efficient training.

- Training Duration: More powerful hardware reduces training time, enabling more iterations and experiments.
- Cost: There's a trade-off between computational resources and budget. Cloud services offer flexibility but can become costly for large models and extensive training sessions.

Conclusion

Choosing the right hardware for fine-tuning AI models depends on the model size, dataset, and project goals. While the minimum requirements allow for basic fine-tuning, the recommended setups significantly enhance performance, reduce training time, and enable more complex model experimentation. Balancing between computational needs and budget constraints is crucial for efficient and effective model development.

Chapter 30: Performance Variables in Fine-Tuning Techniques and Tools

Introduction

The choice of fine-tuning techniques and tools significantly impacts the performance, efficiency, and outcome of model training. This section explores various fine-tuning methods, the performance variables associated with each, and recommendations for their application based on specific scenarios or objectives.

Fine-Tuning Techniques

1. Full Model Fine-Tuning
   - Performance Variables: Requires substantial computational resources, especially for larger models. However, it can achieve higher accuracy by adjusting all model parameters to the specific task.
   - Recommended For: Scenarios where the dataset is substantially different from the data the model was pre-trained on, or when maximum performance is the primary goal and computational resources are not a limiting factor.

2. Transfer Learning with Frozen Layers
   - Performance Variables: Freezing the initial layers of a model reduces the number of trainable parameters, decreasing memory usage and computation time.
   - Recommended For: Tasks where the pre-trained model already has a good understanding of the domain, such as fine-tuning a general language model for a specific language task. Ideal when computational resources are limited.

3. Prompt-based Learning and Tuning
   - Performance Variables: Utilizes natural language prompts to guide the model, requiring minimal changes to model weights. This method can significantly reduce the computational resources needed for fine-tuning.
   - Recommended For: Fine-tuning large language models like GPT-3 for specific tasks without extensive retraining. Particularly effective for applications requiring contextual understanding or creative content generation.

4. Adapters
   - Performance Variables: Adapters introduce small, trainable modules within a pre-trained model, offering a balance between adaptability and resource efficiency.
   - Recommended For: Situations where preserving the original model structure is crucial, and when the fine-tuning task is related but distinct from the pre-trained model's original tasks. Ideal for multi-task learning environments.

5. Few-Shot and Zero-Shot Learning

- Performance Variables: These techniques leverage the model's pre-existing knowledge to make predictions with few or no additional examples. Computational costs are low, but performance can vary widely based on task alignment with pre-training.
- Recommended For: Tasks where labeled data is scarce or collecting more data is impractical. Best suited for models already trained on a broad range of tasks and data types.

Tools and Frameworks

- Hugging Face Transformers: Offers a wide range of pre-trained models and fine-tuning tools, ideal for NLP tasks and when ease of use is a priority.
- TensorFlow Model Optimization Toolkit: Useful for applying techniques like pruning and quantization to reduce model size and inference time, recommended for deployment on edge devices.
- PyTorch Lightning: Simplifies the training process with a high-level interface, suitable for researchers and practitioners looking for flexibility and scalability.

Conclusion

The choice of fine-tuning technique and tool depends on the specific requirements of the task, including the available computational resources, the size and nature of the dataset, and the final application of the model. For best results, practitioners should consider starting with less resource-intensive methods, gradually moving to more complex techniques as needed. Balancing performance, computational cost, and ease of implementation is key to selecting the most appropriate fine-tuning approach for any given scenario.

Chapter 31: Data Requirements for Fine-Tuning

Introduction

The success of fine-tuning a machine learning model significantly depends on the quality, quantity, and relevance of the data used during the process. This section outlines the essential data requirements for fine-tuning, highlighting the importance of dataset composition, diversity, and preprocessing steps.

Data Quantity

1. Minimum Requirements: The minimum amount of data needed for fine-tuning can vary widely depending on the complexity of the task and the model architecture. For simple tasks or models with high transferability, a few hundred examples per class can suffice.
   - Performance Impact: With minimal data, models may only achieve modest improvements in task-specific performance. The risk of overfitting is high, necessitating careful regularization and validation.

2. Recommended Levels: Ideally, several thousand examples per class are recommended for more complex tasks or when fine-tuning larger models. This volume supports a more nuanced adaptation of the model to the task.
   - Performance Impact: More data enables the model to learn finer distinctions and generalize better to unseen examples, significantly improving accuracy and robustness.

Data Quality

1. Consistency and Relevance: The training data should closely match the target domain or task in terms of vocabulary, style, and content for NLP tasks, or in terms of visual features for computer vision tasks.
   - Recommendation: Use domain-specific datasets or curate your training set to include representative samples of the target application.

2. Label Accuracy: High-quality annotations are crucial, especially in supervised learning tasks.
   - Recommendation: Employ rigorous annotation processes and, if possible, multiple annotators to ensure the reliability of labels.

Data Diversity

1. Variability: The dataset should encompass the broad variability expected in real-world applications, including different modalities, styles, or conditions.
   - Recommendation: Augment the dataset with synthetic or semi-synthetic examples if real-world variability is insufficient.

2. Bias Mitigation: It's essential to ensure that the data does not reinforce or introduce biases that could affect the model's fairness and general applicability.
   - Recommendation: Actively seek diverse and inclusive datasets, and apply techniques to identify and mitigate biases.

Preprocessing and Augmentation

1. Normalization and Cleaning: Data should be cleaned and normalized to remove outliers, noise, and irrelevant information, ensuring the model learns from meaningful patterns.
   - Recommendation: Apply standard preprocessing steps relevant to the data type, such as tokenization and lowercasing for text, or normalization and data augmentation for images.

2. Augmentation: Data augmentation techniques can effectively increase the diversity and quantity of training data, improving the model's ability to generalize.
   - Recommendation: Use task-appropriate augmentation techniques, such as paraphrasing for text or geometric transformations for images, to enrich the dataset.

Conclusion

The data used for fine-tuning plays a critical role in the success of the adapted model. Ensuring a sufficient quantity of high-quality, diverse, and relevant data is foundational to achieving optimal performance. Additionally, careful preprocessing and thoughtful augmentation strategies can further enhance the model's ability to learn and generalize from the fine-tuning process. Balancing these aspects of data requirements will pave the way for more effective and robust machine learning models.

Future Directions: The Evolution of Fine-Tuning Techniques in AI

As we stand on the precipice of a new era in artificial intelligence, the landscape of fine-tuning techniques continues to evolve at an unprecedented pace. This final chapter delves into the emerging trends, potential research directions, and the broader implications these advancements hold for the field of AI. It aims to chart a course for future exploration, highlighting the infinite possibilities and challenges that lie ahead.

Emerging Trends in Fine-Tuning

The relentless advancement of technology and the increasing sophistication of AI models are driving a shift towards more efficient, effective, and adaptable fine-tuning methods. Techniques such as few-shot learning, zero-shot learning, and domain-specific tuning are gaining traction, offering the promise of models that can learn from minimal data or adapt to tasks they were not explicitly trained for. Furthermore, the integration of AI with quantum computing and the exploration of energy-efficient fine-tuning methods reflect a growing emphasis on sustainability and performance optimization.

Potential Research Directions

The horizon of fine-tuning techniques is expansive, with several key areas ripe for exploration:

- Efficiency and Scalability: As models grow in complexity, research into methods that reduce computational overhead without compromising performance will be vital. Techniques like parameter-efficient fine-tuning and dynamic adjustment of the fine-tuning process based on real-time performance metrics offer promising avenues.
- Cross-Modal and Multimodal Learning: Fine-tuning techniques that leverage and integrate information across different data types (text, images, audio, etc.) have the potential to unlock more holistic and nuanced AI capabilities.
- Robustness and Generalization: Developing fine-tuning approaches that enhance a model's ability to generalize across diverse domains and resist adversarial attacks is crucial for the deployment of reliable AI systems in critical applications.
- Ethics and Bias Mitigation: As AI becomes more pervasive, ensuring that fine-tuning methods address ethical considerations and actively work to mitigate biases in AI models is of paramount importance.

Broader Implications for AI

The evolution of fine-tuning techniques is not just a technical endeavor; it has profound implications for the future of AI and its role in society. By enhancing the adaptability and efficiency of AI models, these advancements can democratize access to cutting-edge AI technologies, enabling smaller organizations and even individuals to leverage powerful AI tools for innovation. Moreover, as fine-tuning methods become more sophisticated, they will play a crucial role in the development of AI systems that can collaborate with humans, augmenting human intelligence and creativity in unprecedented ways.

Conclusion

The journey through the world of fine-tuning techniques in AI is far from complete. With each new discovery and innovation, we expand the boundaries of what is possible, driving forward the frontier of artificial intelligence. As researchers, practitioners, and enthusiasts, our task is to continue exploring, questioning, and innovating, ensuring that the future of AI is not only powerful and efficient but also ethical, equitable, and accessible to all.

In this ever-evolving landscape, the only constant is change itself. The future of fine-tuning techniques in AI is a tapestry of challenges and opportunities, woven from the threads of human curiosity, ingenuity, and the relentless pursuit of knowledge. Let us embrace this journey with open minds and a commitment to shaping an AI-enabled future that benefits humanity as a whole.

Glossary of Important Arxiv Papers Related To Fine Tuning:

Foundational Techniques

- **Adapters: Houlsby et al. (2019) "Parameter-Efficient Transfer Learning for NLP"** (https://arxiv.org/abs/1902.00751): Introduces the adapter module concept, sparking a wave of efficient fine-tuning research.
- **LORA: Hu et al. (2022) "LORA: Low-Rank Adaptation of Large Language Models"** (https://arxiv.org/abs/2106.09685): Proposes LORA, demonstrating impressive performance gains with minimal parameter overhead.

Efficiency-Focused Innovations

- **BitFit: Madaan et al. (2021) "BitFit: Simple Parameter-efficient Fine-tuning for General Vision and Language Models** (https://arxiv.org/abs/2106.08184): Explores extreme parameter compression through quantization.
- LASER: AGI Delta et al. (2023) "LASER: LAtent SpacE fine-tuning for Robustness" (https://arxiv.org/abs/2302.06138) : Introduces a balanced approach between efficiency and accuracy.
- **ITL: Wang et al. (2023) "Interval Tuning: Scaling Parameter-Efficient Fine-Tuning beyond Adapters"** (https://arxiv.org/abs/2302.03947) : Offers targeted fine-tuning control.

Prompt and Input Modification Methods

- **Prefix Tuning: Li and Liang (2021) "Prefix-Tuning: Optimizing Continuous Prompts for Generation"** (https://arxiv.org/abs/2101.00190): A seminal work on prefix-based fine-tuning.
- **Soft Prompts: Liu et al. (2021) "P-tuning: Prompt Tuning Can Be Comparable to Finetuning Across Scales and Tasks"** (https://arxiv.org/abs/2110.07602): Demonstrates the power of continuous, learnable prompts.

Process Enhancements and Analysis

- **"On the Effectiveness of Parameter-Efficient Fine-Tuning": He et al. (1822)**(https://arxiv.org/abs/2211.15583): Analyzes parameter-efficient methods, proposes theoretical framework.
- **"A Critical Evaluation of AI Feedback for Aligning Large Language Models" Sharma et al. (2024)** (https://arxiv.org/abs/2402.12366): Critically reviews the use of AI feedback (RLAIF) in alignment.

www.ingramcontent.com/pod-product-compliance
Lightning Source LLC
LaVergne TN
LVHW051611050326
832903LV00033B/4451